## LOOKING AT HISTORY:
## FROM CAVEMEN TO VIKINGS

By means of over two hundred pictures and vivid text, R. J. Unstead tells the story of life in Britain from the cavemen to the Viking conquest. He tells about people's homes, the sort of food they ate, the way they dressed and the amusements they enjoyed. He also tells you about the Roman conquest of Britain and the Roman influence on British life, and about the later invasions by the Angles and Saxons and then the Vikings.

FROM CAVEMEN TO VIKINGS is the first book in the famous LOOKING AT HISTORY series.

'An excellent introduction to the concrete details of the past.'

*Times Literary Supplement*

3 bcd

Other books by R. J. UNSTEAD

THE STORY OF BRITAIN: BEFORE THE NORMAN CONQUEST
THE STORY OF BRITAIN: IN THE MIDDLE AGES
THE STORY OF BRITAIN: IN TUDOR AND STUART TIMES
THE STORY OF BRITAIN: FROM WILLIAM OF ORANGE TO WORLD WAR II
SOME KINGS AND QUEENS
ROYAL ADVENTURERS
PRINCES AND REBELS
DISCOVERERS AND ADVENTURERS
GREAT LEADERS
HEROES AND SAINTS
PEOPLE IN HISTORY: FROM CARACTACUS TO ALFRED
LOOKING AT HISTORY: THE MIDDLE AGES
LOOKING AT HISTORY: TUDORS AND STUARTS
LOOKING AT HISTORY: QUEEN ANNE TO QUEEN ELIZABETH II

and published by CAROUSEL BOOKS

# LOOKING AT HISTORY

R. J. UNSTEAD

## Book I
## FROM CAVEMEN TO VIKINGS

Consultant editor: Anne Wood

**CAROUSEL BOOKS**
A DIVISION OF TRANSWORLD PUBLISHERS LTD

LOOKING AT HISTORY: FROM CAVEMEN TO VIKINGS
A CAROUSEL BOOK      0 552 54067 6

Originally published in Great Britain by
A. & C. Black Ltd.

PRINTING HISTORY
A. & C. Black edition published 1953
A. & C. Black edition reissued 1961
A. & C. Black edition reprinted 1972
Carousel edition published 1975

Carousel Books are published by Transworld Publishers, Ltd, Cavendish House, 57-59
Uxbridge Road, Ealing, London W5

Printed by James Paton Ltd., Paisley.

# CONTENTS

# ACKNOWLEDGMENTS

Most of the drawings reproduced in this book are by J. C. B. Knight. Others are by Caton Woodville, Cecile Walton, Pearl Binder, E. Dalang, Gladys M. Rees and Amédée Forestier, from his book *The Roman Soldier*. Drawings of costume are taken from Mary G. Houston's *Ancient Greek, Roman and Byzantine Costume and Decoration* and Iris Brooke's *Costume of the Early Middle Ages*. The maps are drawn by J. H. L. Williams.

The cave painting on page 17 is reproduced from *The Progress of Early Man* by kind permission of Stuart Piggott. The picture reproduced on page 60, *St Augustine preaching to the English*, is by Stephen B. Carlill.

As very few contemporary records of this age exist, drawings, with the exception of those on pages 66 and 67, are imaginative reconstructions, made after careful research.

# PEOPLE OF THE STONE AGE

Long, long ago, before there were any roads or houses or books, or even fields and hedges, our land was covered with thick forests.

Here are some of the fierce wild animals which lived in the jungle:

hippopotamus

rhinoceros

lion

elk

hyena

elephant

bear

There were also animals like these, which have now died out. Some of their bones have been dug up. These bones, which have turned as hard as stone, are called fossils.

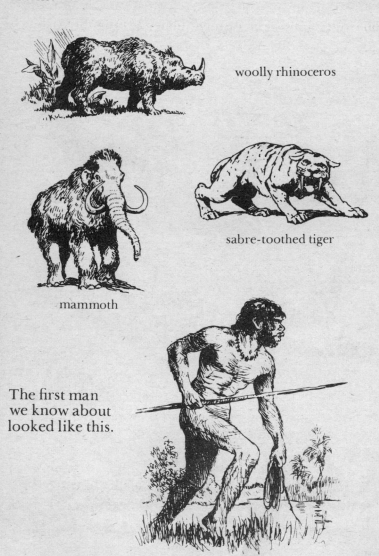

woolly rhinoceros

sabre-toothed tiger

mammoth

The first man
we know about
looked like this.

The weather was very hot and he did not wear clothes. We think he ate berries and fruit and the meat of any little animals he could catch.

He drank from the streams. He often hid in the trees from wild animals, or found a shelter among the rocks.

The weather became colder and colder. Some animals, like lions, tigers and bison, went away from our country. (They could do this because, long ago, our land was joined to France.)

Early man felt cold too. He was not as big and strong as the animals, but he was much more clever.

He wrapped himself in skins and started to make things.

Early man made a home in a cave

He liked his cave to be near a river and near to a place where he could find flints.

He had no knives to cut with and he had never heard of iron, so he used sharp stones called flints, and he learned to chip them into many shapes.

At first he made a sort of knife called a hand-axe. He then made scrapers and borers (to make holes in wood).

His wife used the scraper to clean the underside of animal skins, so that they could be worn as clothes in the cold winter.

Next, they made a very important thing, which no animal has ever made — they made a fire.

They learned to rub a stick in a groove of another piece of wood, until it grew warmer and warmer, and at last made a tiny flame. This was a job for Caveman's wife.

She also found that if she struck certain stones, sparks would fly out and set fire to dry grass.

Everyone tried to keep the fire alight. The children gathered wood.

They started to cook their food by holding lumps of meat on sticks near the fire.

The cavemen were hunters. They did not know how to grow food, nor how to keep animals.

Sometimes the wild animals would move to new feeding grounds. Then Caveman and his family would follow them. The hunters went great distances in search of food, living where they could among bushes and rocks. In winter they went back to the family's cave.

It was a hard life, trying to catch and kill the big animals. They dug pits for traps. They made spears and wooden handles for the stone axes.

Later, they made bows and arrows.

The animals gave them food to eat, skins to wear, and from the bones they made needles and fish-hooks.

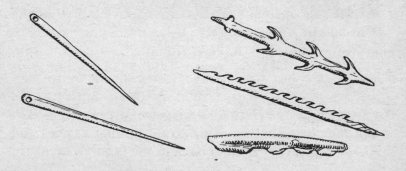

The cavemen made their first boats by cutting down trees near the river with their big stone axes. Then they would hollow a tree-trunk into the shape of a boat, using flints and fire to do so.

They liked fish and went fishing with a spear. They also used bone fish-hooks on lines made from animal sinews and strong grasses.

Some people lived by the sea and ate shellfish. They left great piles of shells behind.

Some cavemen painted pictures on the walls of their caves. For paint they used brown and yellow earth and soot from the fire.

They drew the animals they wanted to kill when out hunting. Animals gave them all they needed — food and clothes—so they drew them very carefully.

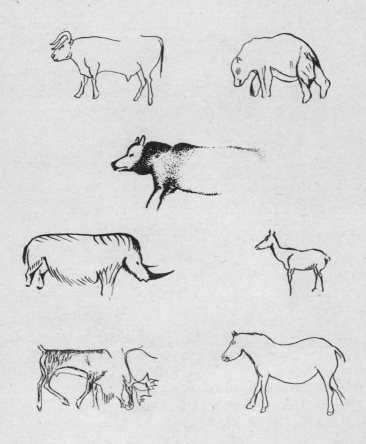

It was a kind of magic to paint pictures in the dark cave.

Hundreds of years went by and the weather became warmer. Then the forests were not quite so big and there were grassy hills.

Life became a little easier, but men had to spend nearly all their time getting enough to eat.

The men still went hunting for deer and bison, bears, wolves and wild boar.

They had dogs now to help them. Dogs were the first tame animals.

The next tame animals were sheep, cows and pigs. People began to look after flocks and herds instead of always going hunting for food.

When the animals moved about to find grass, the people moved with them and lived in camps of little huts.

The first hut had a pole in the middle and some long sticks tied to the top, which were covered with skins. It was only a shelter and the fire was outside.

# THE NEW STONE AGE

The early men were learning all the time.

They became very clever at making flint tools and even polished them.

They dug deep into the chalk to find flints, using pickaxes made from stags' horns.

The women made clay pots and bowls to hold milk. They shaped the clay with their hands and baked the pots in a fire of brushwood.

Men began to build larger huts. These had a low wall of stones, with a gap for the door. There was a pole in the middle and the roof was made of grassy turf.

The fire was made on a flat stone and the smoke went out through a hole in the roof. Some flat stones covered with skins made a bed.

If there were no stones to make a wall, they set up a ring of posts and tied poles from them to the big post in the middle.

The walls were made of a kind of basketwork called wattle, smeared all over with wet clay. This kept the wind out.

When a group of huts had been built, a long fence was put right round them to keep out wild animals and enemies. Inside the fence were houses, pens for the animals, hay-ricks and poles for drying grass and a dew-pond.

The animals were brought in at night. In the morning, the flocks were let out to feed on the grassy hills.

Several families living together in this way made a tribe, which was led by a Chief.

Here is the Chief
of one of these early tribes
with his spear
and his hunting-dog.

This was still the Stone Age and men did not know about God, but they worshipped the Sun and Moon.

They built rings of huge stones for their gods.

There is one at Stonehenge on Salisbury Plain.

It is so old that no one is quite sure how it was made. Perhaps they raised the great stones like this.

When men had to travel, they walked along the tops of low hills, because the valleys were full of forests with wild animals in them. So they made grassy roads, like the Icknield Way, which led to Stonehenge.

The tribes were often fighting. They built forts on the hilltops so that they could keep a watch for enemies.

# PEOPLE OF THE BRONZE AND IRON AGES

## BRONZE

Men from the East came to live in our land about this time and they brought a new metal with them. It was bronze, which is a mixture of two metals, copper and tin, heated together.

Bronze gave men sharper tools and weapons which did not break and which could be made quickly. When a bronze axe became blunt, it could be hammered until it was sharp again.

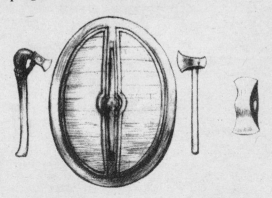

Spears, shields, axes and the first swords were made.

Homes were still round huts. The girls and women now had cooking pots and bowls made of bronze, in many shapes and patterns.

The men became farmers. They cut the grass and dried it, to make hay for the winter. This was dried on poles.

They had cows and sheep, and the boys looked after the pigs near the forest.

With a wooden plough they scratched the earth and planted corn. As you can see, they used oxen for ploughing.

When the corn was ripe, the women ground it into flour between stones. Then they made bread and flat cakes, cooking them on the hot stones by the fire.

About this time men began to make wheels and to train horses to pull carts and war chariots.

To cross rivers, and for fishing, they made round boats, of basketwork, covered with skin, called coracles.

These boats were so light that a man could carry one on his back.

You can still see these round boats in some parts of Wales.

## IRON

After many more years, people called Celts came from over the sea and brought another metal with them called iron. It made better knives, swords and tools because it was harder than bronze, which was still used for many things such as pins, brooches and bowls.

Twisting wool into long threads is called spinning. This was mostly done by girls.

The stick in the girl's right hand is called the spindle and the round weight on the end is the whorl. On her shoulder is the distaff with a roll of wool. She twists the wool with her fingers until she has a piece long enough to tie on to the spindle stick, which spins round and twists the wool into thread.

The threads were made into cloth by weaving. You can see in the picture that some threads are fixed down the frame to keep them straight, and the girl weaves her threads in and out across them. In this way they made woollen cloth.

Flax, a plant with a pretty blue flower, grew wild in the woods and fields.

The Bronze and Iron Age people found that if they soaked flax plants in the river and dried them in the sun, they could pick out the silky part of the stems and spin it into thread. This was made into a cloth called linen.

They dyed their linen and woollen clothes with dyes made from plants and tree bark.

At first, the Bronze Age people just wrapped the cloth round themselves and fastened it with pins and brooches.

The girl has sewn her dress under the arms and she has a belt with a bronze buckle. Her hair is worn in a net, with long pins.

This man wears a short tunic and a woollen cap. His cloak has no sleeves. They both wear skin shoes.

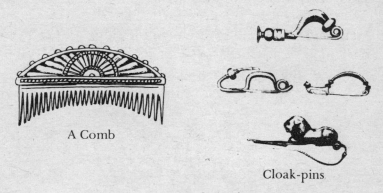

A Comb

Cloak-pins

The bronze buckles and brooches were beautifully made. Some ornaments were made of gold, which was found in Britain at this time.

## A LAKE VILLAGE

Sometimes, to be safe from enemies, men built their homes in a lake or marsh.

Men made an island by driving poles into the mud and by piling up earth and stones until they could build huts of wattle. Then they put a fence all round.

There was a Lake Village at Glastonbury in Somerset.

Each hut had a pole in the middle to hold up the roof, and there was a flat hearth-stone on the floor. When this heavy stone sank into the soft ground, a new stone was put on top. As many as ten stones have been found on top of one another.

The Lake-dwellers went ashore in boats to look after their fields and animals, but returned to the Lake Village at night.

# THE ANCIENT BRITONS

The Ancient Britons were also called Celts and they came from across the sea.

They were quite clever people and lived in tribes with Chiefs, and sometimes Kings and Queens, but the tribes were always fighting each other.

Their huts were like the Celtic homes, but their clothes were woven in bright colours. The men wore tartan kilts or long loose trousers. You can see they also had helmets and cloaks. Some tribes were very skilful at making beautiful jewellery and pottery.

The women wore short sleeves and a band on their hair. Both men and women wore plaits.

Here is one of their war-chariots. Notice the curved knife which sticks out from the wheel.

The Ancient Britons were good farmers. Here they are working in their narrow fields on a hillside, which has a fort on the top.

Some men now had their own special jobs, doing the work at which they were best. Some were shepherds or bee-keepers, makers of harness or ploughs or leather buckets. Some made boats and others swords and shields.

There were rich chiefs and poor men, and slaves, captured in battle.

Here is a Chief being rowed across a lake. His helmet is made of bronze and his shield has a pattern made of red enamel studs.

Some men were traders. They travelled along the wide paths (like the Icknield Way) to buy and sell goods such as cloth, corn, tin, skins and ornaments.

A Gallic Chief

They used iron bars and gold coins for money, and even went across in boats to Gaul (the old name for France). The Britons were friendly to the Gauls.

Traders from the East, with dark faces, came to Britain to buy tin and gold, hunting-dogs and skins. Their fine cloth of bright colours pleased the Britons.

These traders were called Phoenicians. They came from Carthage, in North Africa, and were the greatest traders before the Romans. They sailed as far as the Baltic Sea to buy amber.

Here you can see some Phoenician traders bartering with a British family.

This picture shows some Phoenicians building a ship for a trading voyage.

The Ancient Britons were not Christians. They worshipped the Sun, the Moon and Nature.

Their priests were Druids, who said that the Oak and the Mistletoe were sacred. When the Mistletoe was cut, white bulls, and even people captured in war, were killed as sacrifices.

The island of Anglesey was the Druids' holy island.

When the Romans came, they soon found that the Druids were leaders of the Britons. They went across to Anglesey and killed them.

# THE ROMANS

One day, some years before Jesus was born, the Romans came to Britain.

Julius Caesar

The Ancient Britons had been helping the Gauls across the sea to fight against the Roman general, Julius Caesar. This made him angry and he brought some of his soldiers across the Channel to punish the Britons.

Here you see a British warrior watching the arrival of the Romans.

After a fierce fight on the beach, they landed at Deal.

The Britons promised to pay some money to Rome and the Romans soon went away.

One hundred years afterwards, the Romans came again, and this time they meant to stay.

They came in long ships like this, and after many battles they defeated the Britons and ruled over them.

The Britons fought bravely under King Caractacus, and Boadicea, Queen of the Iceni tribe, but the Romans wore armour and were better soldiers, because they always obeyed their captains.

These pictures show the uniforms of Roman soldiers.

A Roman Legionary    A Standard Bearer    A Centurion    A Roman Guard

You can see the short sword, long spear, curved shield and armour worn over a leather jacket.

There were also archers and horsemen.

The soldiers followed their standard bearers into battle.

The Romans brought machines like these to attack the forts.

Battering Ram

Stone-throwing Engine

Two Catapults

The Romans built roads which were as straight as possible, so that soldiers could march quickly to any place where they were needed.

Notice the heavy load which each legionary had to carry.

These roads were built in layers, so cleverly and strongly, that they lasted for hundreds of years.

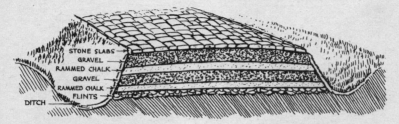

Because they were clever and hard-working, and did most things better than the Britons, they soon ruled over all the land, except the North. Here the fierce Picts and Scots were troublesome, so the Romans built a great wall across the country to keep them out.

Roman Officers on Hadrian's Wall

Then there was peace and the Britons grew used to the Romans and copied their ways.

A big Roman house in the country was called a villa.

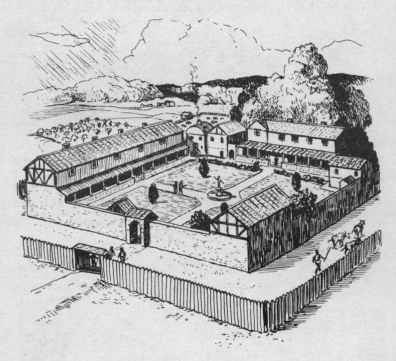

It was built of brick and had a tiled roof. Most of the villas were in the south of England.

A Roman villa was built round a courtyard with a fountain or pool in the middle. There were many rooms, kitchens, larders and baths, as well as rooms for the slaves. A long covered porch, or verandah, with a low wall and pillars, was built along the front of the villa to keep the rooms cool in summer. (You can see the verandah clearly on page 51.)

Here is the dining-room in the villa of a rich Roman.

The floor was made of tiny coloured stones set in cement. The walls were painted in pretty colours or covered with marble. There was glass in the windows.

The Romans did not sit round the table, but lay on couches to eat their food. It was good manners to do this. The plates and dishes were made of red pottery, glass and silver.

The delicious food was cooked by slaves over a charcoal fire in the kitchen.

The room, you can see, was heated in a clever way. Underneath the floor was a space, because it was built on little pillars. A fire outside the wall sent hot air under the floor and up the sides of the walls.

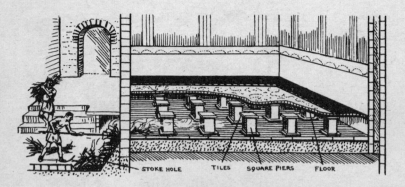

STOKE HOLE    TILES    SQUARE PIERS    FLOOR

The Romans loved washing and bathing, so in every town and in big villas there were baths.

There were usually three bathrooms—a warm one, a hot one, where slaves would rub their masters all over with sweet oil, and a big cold bath to swim in.

There are still Roman baths in the city of Bath, in Avon.

The Roman towns in Britain were full of fine buildings and temples. These were built round a big square called the Forum, where people would come to talk and to buy in the market.

An Aqueduct        A Temple        An Archway

Aqueducts were bridges for bringing water to towns.

Here is a busy street scene. The stepping-stones for crossing over in wet weather were placed so that a cart could pass.

Important Romans dressed in a long robe called a toga. It was made of white wool or linen, with a purple border. Underneath they wore a tunic.

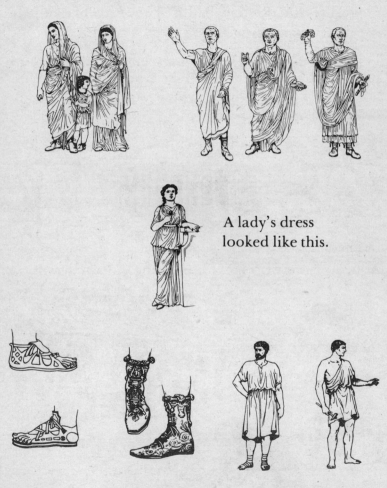

A lady's dress looked like this.

The poor people and the slaves still wore clothes rather like the Britons'.

Everyone wore sandals or heavy shoes.

SENATVS·PO
IMP·CAESARI·I
TRAIANO·AV(
MAXIMO·TRIB

The Romans taught the Britons to read and write. They did beautiful writing.

The children would write on wax with a pencil called a stylus. This was a piece of wood, iron or ivory, with a sharp point at one end. At the other end was a knob to smooth out mistakes.

The Romans liked to go out and enjoy themselves.

They would go to the amphitheatre or to the circus to see chariot races.

They also liked to see men fighting wild beasts or each other. These men were called gladiators. It was a cruel sport, for one man was usually killed.

A Gladiator

After a long time, the Romans and the Britons became Christians and the first churches in Britain were built.

Life was peaceful, for the Romans made good laws.

The children did not go to school, but if their parents were rich they had a tutor or teacher at the villa.

The boys had to learn many of the same things as we do, and also to ride a pony and to use a little sword.

The girls learnt to sew and to keep house. They played with dolls and balls and a game called knuckle-bones. They always obeyed their father.

Here is a Roman lady, carried in a litter by her slaves.

The Romans ruled over a great Empire, of which Britain was only a tiny part. Wherever they went the Romans brought peace, good laws, good roads and fine buildings.

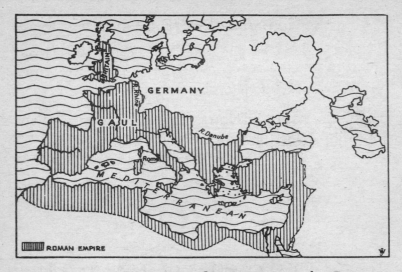

After they had been here for 400 years, the Romans went away. Their homes in Italy were being attacked by fierce tribes and every soldier was needed.

The Britons were sad when they went, for they had no soldiers of their own to protect them from the sea-raiders, who were growing bolder in their attacks upon the coast.

# THE ANGLES AND SAXONS

The Angles, Saxons and Jutes had been attacking our shores for many years. After the Romans had gone, they came more often to plunder and steal.

They came across the North Sea from Germany in their long ships, which had one sail and many oars.

The Anglo-Saxons, as they were called, were tall, fair-haired men, armed with swords and spears and round shields. As you can see, they also wore armour, rings of metal sewn on to a leather jacket.

They loved fighting and were cruel, fierce heathens who did not know about Jesus Christ. Their gods were Woden and Thor.

Woden

Thor

At first they would sail up the rivers, burn the towns and villas and steal everything they could carry off. They would then return home.

Later on, some of them did not go back after a raid but stayed to make homes here. They killed the Britons or drove them into the hills and mountains of Wales and Cornwall.

The Anglo-Saxons did not understand the Roman ways and would not live in their towns, so the villas and streets and baths were soon forgotten. They fell into ruins and became covered over with weeds.

The Anglo-Saxons called their new country Angleland.

When they built a house they first made a frame of wood and filled in the spaces with basketwork, grass and mud.

All round the village was a high fence to keep the herds safe at night from enemies and the wild animals in the forests—wolves, foxes and boars.

The biggest house was the Hall, which was the Chief's house, and he lived there with his warriors.

It was long, wide and smoky, with the fire on a stone in the middle, so that smoke had to go out through a hole in the roof.

The windows were slits called eye-holes.

On the walls were shields and antlers. The floor was dirty and covered with rushes from the river banks.

Sometimes the oxen were kept at one end of the Hall.

The Anglo-Saxons loved eating and drinking and would often have feasts in the Hall. The food was cooked over the fire in the middle; the meat was roasted and eaten with bread.

A minstrel or gleeman

They drank ale and mead—a kind of beer made sweet with honey—from great goblets and drinking horns.

After the feast a minstrel would play his harp and sing songs of battles and heroes.

At last the warriors would go to sleep on the benches or near the fire. The Chief and his wife would go to bed in a separate hut called a bower, or in a large bed built close to the wall.

Here are some more Anglo-Saxons, wearing shirt and breeches, with a tunic on top.

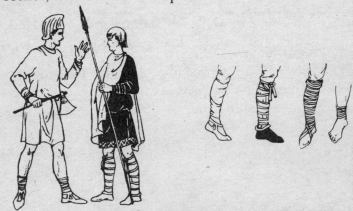

Cloaks were fastened with beautiful brooches. Helmets were made of leather and iron.

Their leggings have cross-garters of leather joined to their shoes. Shoes did not yet have heels.

Most warriors carried a spear and a battleaxe for throwing. Chiefs or Thanes had swords.

Their round shields were made of wood covered with leather and painted.

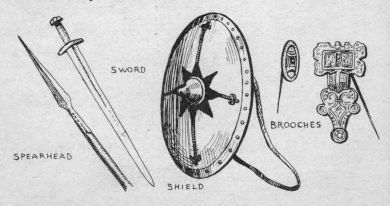

SWORD

SPEARHEAD

SHIELD

BROOCHES

The women wore a linen vest and a long dress with a girdle. On top was a mantle, a long piece of cloth with a hole for the head.

The Anglo-Saxons loved bright colours and were good weavers.

They were good farmers, too, and grew wheat, barley, oats and rye. You can see that they used a sickle for cutting the corn.

They kept herds of cattle and sheep and many pigs. The children helped to look after the animals, and they played battles with toy spears and axes.

After about 200 years, St. Augustine came from Rome with some brave monks, to teach the Anglo-Saxons about Christ.

King Ethelbert of Kent, whose Queen, Bertha, was already a Christian, made his people give up their old gods and become Christians.

St. Augustine built a church at Canterbury.

The Britons, who had been driven to the west by the Saxons, had never forgotten the teachings of Christ, which they learned in Roman days. Some had gone to Ireland, and St. Columba and Aidan spread the news of Jesus in Scotland and the North.

St. Augustine's Chair
Canterbury Cathedral

When they became Christians, the Anglo-Saxons were not quite so rough. The monks would teach them and some of the children went to school. The monks taught them in Latin.

The monks were almost the only people who could read and write. They used quill pens and wrote on parchment or vellum. This writing took them a long time and it is difficult for us to read it nowadays.

Bede was a famous monk who lived in a monastery at Jarrow, in the north of England.

He is often called the "Father of English History", because he wrote, not only hymns, prayers and lives of the saints, but the first history of England.

When he was very old, the monks came to his bedside and wrote down what he told them.

A Saxon Church

Churches, usually of wood, were built in the Saxon villages, and the whole land was becoming peaceful, when suddenly, about the year 800, bands of fierce raiders began to attack our coasts.

They were the Danes, and they came not only from Denmark, but also from Norway, where there was not enough land for the warriors.

# THE DANES

The Danes came across the North Sea, just as the Anglo-Saxons had done. They came in long ships which had one square sail and many oars on each side.

The Danes were also called Vikings or Norsemen. They usually wore horned or winged helmets.

They were fierce and cruel, and came to burn the Saxons' villages and to steal all they could carry off. They were armed with spears and two-handed battle-axes.

They would sail up a river or creek, and leave their ships to steal horses and ride round the countryside killing and burning.

In time, like the Anglo-Saxons, they made their homes here. They drove the Saxons out of part of the country and took it for themselves.

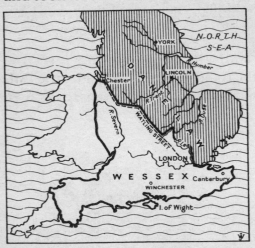

King Alfred

King Alfred, Saxon king of Wessex, fought them and beat them in a great battle, but he could not drive them right away and had to let them have part of the country, called the Danelaw.

Alfred the Great was a wise and brave king. He liked learning and started a few schools.

He made the people obey his laws and build better houses and churches.

He repaired the Roman town of London, but Winchester was the capital city.

This picture shows Alfred as a little boy being taught to read by his mother.

He built ships to fight the Danes in order to keep them out of Wessex.

The Danes were heathens at first. Their gods were Odin, Thor and Freya, and they believed that men who died in battle went to Valhalla and feasted with the gods.

The Danish dress was rather like the Saxons', as you can see in this picture of a Viking Chief and his lady.

Presently the Danes and the Saxons settled down together and became Christians. About the year 980 there were fresh raids by the Northmen.

This is an old drawing of Canute, a Dane, who became King of England—a wise, strong king. After he had defeated Edmund Ironside, Canute ruled a sea-empire that stretched from England to Denmark. There was peace and trading in his reign.

At this time many churches were built of stone instead of wood.

This is the tower of a Saxon church, which was built so strongly, that it is still standing.

King Edward the Confessor built an Abbey at Westminster.

After him came Harold.

Harold was King of England before William the Conqueror seized his Kingdom in 1066.

England now had many towns and villages. Much of the forest was cut down, and most people were farmers, but the Danes liked trading as well.

There were not many roads, and very few people went on journeys.

There were monasteries in many places and a church in every village.

The King ruled the land with his earls and bishops to help him. The soldiers of his bodyguard were called Thegns or Thanes. They were land-owners.

They enjoyed themselves hunting and feasting, but the farming was done by the Freemen, the Husbandmen and the Serfs (or Thralls).

The men who gave the King advice and who sometimes chose a new King were called the Witan, which means a meeting of the wise men.

Winchester was the capital of Wessex and England, but London was now beginning to grow big and rich.

Houses were still made of wood, with thatched roofs.

Inside, there was one large room where the husbandman, his family and their cow all lived together.

# LET'S TRY TO REMEMBER

# LET'S TRY TO REMEMBER

Homes were like this:

1. Caves

2. Stone Age round huts

3. Lake huts

4. Celtic huts with stockade

5. Roman villa

6. Anglo-Saxon settlement

# Weapons

### Flint

### Roman

### Bronze

### Anglo-Saxon

### Iron

### Danish

They wore clothes like these:

Caveman

Roman soldier

Man of the New Stone Age

People of the Bronze Age

Viking

Ancient Briton

Saxons

People lived in caves,

then

they made round huts,

then

they lived in lake dwellings.

Then

they lived in houses grouped together, with a fence around them. They were Celts or Ancient Britons.

Then

the Romans came,

and conquered.

They built towns and became Christians.

After the Romans had gone away,

the Angles, Saxons and Jutes came.

They were heathens and very fierce.

St. Augustine taught them to be Christians.

Then

the Danes (or Vikings) came.

They were heathens at first.

King Alfred fought the Danes.

The Saxons and Danes settled down together

as Christian people.

## EVERYDAY LIFE IN THE VIKING AGE
*by* JACQUELINE SIMPSON                                    30p

552 54011 0                                    Carousel Non-Fiction

The Vikings were not merely plunderers and marauders, but also a civilised people with a culture of their own — as recent excavations have shown. Jacqueline Simpson provides a full and fascinating account of their way of life covering their domestic life as well as their better-known overseas adventures.


## TALES TOLD BY THE FOSSILS — Vols. I and II
*by* CARROLL LANE FENTON                                 30p

### Vol. I — UNEARTHING LIFE'S PAST

552 54046 3                                    Carousel Non-Fiction

This volume explains what fossils are, how they are found and how they divide the earth's history into an orderly series of ages.

### Vol. I I — FROM DINOSAURS TO MAN

552 54047 1

Traces the history of life from the late Triassic period, 230 million years ago when lizard-hipped dinosaurs lived up until 100,000 years ago when mankind had developed from "ape-man" to "Neanderthal man".


## HEROES AND SAINTS
*by* R. J. UNSTEAD                                        25p

552 54050 1                                    Carousel Non-Fiction

What kind of men and women became Heroes and Saints? What dangers and hardships did they have to overcome? R. J. Unstead has chosen some of the most courageous heroes and saints — Julius Caesar and the Emperor Hadrian are among them — and tells their stories.

## ALL ABOUT KING ARTHUR
*by* GEOFFREY ASHE                                        30p

552 54039 0                          Carousel Non-Fiction

Arthur, King of Britain, became a national hero between the years of 1150 and 1200. The real ruler during most of that time was Henry II. But the legendary monarch was soon more widely renowned than the actual one . . . and his fame in romance has continued ever since.

How did the Arthurian Legend begin, and in what forms have writers and poets presented it over the ages? Even more important are the questions: Did King Arthur and his knights ever exist at all? How far are the stories true, how far are they invented? If any of the things happened, when did they happen?

Geoffrey Ashe explores both these paths. He traces the Arthur of fiction from the Middle Ages to the present day; he also tells the historical and archaeological facts of all that is known about the King.


## EVERYDAY LIFE IN PREHISTORIC TIMES
*by* MARJORIE and C. B. H. QUENNELL                  25p

Series                                   Carousel Non-Fiction

This series presents a picture in words of how our forefathers lived in their prehistoric world, moving out of their caves into the earliest settlements; discovering metals; making fires; building and construction the first organized villages. The EVERYDAY LIFE series follows them, detailing their development into civilisation as we know it.

## THE STORY OF BRITAIN
*by* R. J. UNSTEAD                                              30p

Series                                    Carousel Non-Fiction

A country is forged by its history, the battles and intrigues of by-gone ages laying the foundations of today. From its beginnings as an island to the end of the Second World War, this series is the record of the men and women who played a role in shaping the character of England now. It traces the emergence of England as a nation.

## GREAT LEADERS
*by* R. J. UNSTEAD                                              30p

552 54044 7                              Carousel Non-Fiction

'A small red-headed pupil, the naughtiest boy in the class,' reported one teacher. The boy he was talking about was Winston Churchill!

Winston Churchill had to face many setbacks and disappointments before he became a 'great leader'. So did Robert Baden-Powell who started the Boy Scouts; Amy Johnson who was the first woman to fly the Atlantic; and Lord Nuffield who founded Morris Motors. These are just a few of the great leaders that R. J. Unstead has written about in this book.

........................................................................................................................................

All these books are available at your bookshop or can be ordered direct from Transworld Publishers Ltd., Cash Sales Dept., P.O. Box 11, Falmouth, Cornwall.

Please send full name and address together with cheque or postal order — no currency and allow 10p per book to cover the cost of postage and packing (plus 5p each for additional copies).

........................................................................................................................................

If you would like to receive a newsletter telling you about our new children's books, send your name and address to Gillian Osband, Transworld Publishers Ltd., 57/59 Uxbridge Road, Ealing, London, W5, and mention "CHILDRENS NEWSLETTER".